# NOTE-TAKING SKILLS EXAM SU

## HOW TO TAKE SMART VISUAL NOTES AND BECOME AN A-STUDENT

Printed by CreateSpace, An Amazon.com Company

ISBN-13: 978-1532846052

ISBN-10: 1532846053

## JONNIE TANYA

Copyright Rank Books 2016

www.rankbooks.com

# Contents

| | |
|---|---|
| Introduction | 3 |
| Chapter 1 | 5 |
| Why take notes? | 5 |
| Chapter 2 | 7 |
| Why most people take notes the wrong way? | 7 |
| Chapter 3 | 10 |
| Better listening equals BETTER note-taking | 10 |
| Chapter 4 | 17 |
| Effective note-taking techniques | 17 |
| - Cornell Note-taking System | |
| - The Outlining Method | |
| - T-Charts and 3-Column Charts | |
| - The Concept Mapping Method | |
| - Fishbone Map | |
| - Use symbols and abbreviations in your notes | |
| - Visual Notes Quick Guide | |
| Chapter 5 | 49 |
| What To Do With The First And last Few Pages Of Your Notebook? | 49 |
| RESOURCES | |

# INTRODUCTION

Note-taking is an essential part of learning at school and at work.

For a student, having smart note-taking skill can make a difference between an 'A' student or a 'C' student. When used at work, a person who has better note-taking skill can work more efficiently and hence get a higher chance for a promotion.

The small effects of good note-taking skills add up. Your success or failure in school or at work may depend on it. If you take great notes, you can revise more efficiently and you can better prepare your examination. You can reference important information without having to ask your friends or teachers again the next day or go looking for the information from various text books.

Great note-taking skill is more than just taking down points accurately. It is about taking notes intelligently and organizing it in a way that facilitates recall, referencing and even creating new ideas. It is also about active listening and information processing skills.

Note-taking skill can be applied not just during lectures or seminars but also when making notes while reading a book.

## What Makes Good Lecture Notes?

1. Notes must be neat and readable

2. Notes must show the main points of the lecture

3. Notes must show the relationship of the details to the main points

4. Notes must contain visuals that can quickly highlight important points, concepts and ideas

5. Notes must point you the way to get more information if needed

This book covers three major components of taking great notes:

- Part 1: Actively listening skills
- Part 2: Note-taking methods and strategies
- Part 3: Recall And Processing of Notes

# CHAPTER 1

# WHY TAKE NOTES?

Effective note-taking skill is so important but not everyone is taught the right skills from young. For most of us, taking notes means copying as much as you can and as fast as you can. But, there are better methods to record down what you hear to facilitate knowledge retention and process information more effectively.

We take notes when listening to a lecture in a classroom, during an online lesson or even watching a video related to the subject of study. But did you ever ask if those notes you have taken make sense to you?

Is the information captured useful? Note-taking is a process of filtering, classifying and connecting information as well and not merely to record information on what has been said.

Dr. Walter Paulk, director of Cornell University's reading and study center and creator of the Cornell Note-taking System, estimated that 60% of content learned is forgotten within 2 weeks without notes. However, having a note-taking system that requires review and critical thinking results in almost 90-100% retention.

Taking notes aids your comprehension and retention. Researchers found that if important information was contained in notes, it had a 34% chance of being remembered (Howe, 1970, in Longman and Atkinson, 1999). Information not found in notes had only a 5% chance of being remembered.  Your notes should represent a concise and complete outline of the most important points and ideas, especially those considered most important by the presenter.  They can also clarify ideas not fully understood in the text or elaborate on material that the text mentions only briefly.  Your notes may be the only written reference you will have on the information discussed.  Although we have ipads, smartphones and tablets with writing apps, you can simply write, make mathematical and scientific notations, and draw faster on paper than you can typing words out or even drawing on a tablet.

# CHAPTER 2

# WHY MOST PEOPLE TAKE NOTES THE WRONG WAY?

Many people do not realize that they take notes the wrong way.

Studies conducted by international transcription and translation specialists found that the most common mistakes of workers was in attempting to take notes verbatim; they neither could transcribe every word or neatly enough to read their own handwriting.

Global Lingo, a UK business specializing in professional transcription and translation services, polled more than 2000 employees working in several different industries. More than two-thirds of those polled said that they did take notes at work and more than half take notes on a weekly basis.

However, of those who took notes at work, 90% 'regularly' took notes poorly or incorrectly. Based on this survey, the average worker spent 32 minutes a week trying to decipher, rewrite or otherwise correct bad notes. This adds up to 24.7 hours lost per working year per employee. Considering the median hourly wage, bad notes are costing UK businesses almost £4 billion per year in lost productivity.

Note-taking is not a skill that is easily acquired overnight. It requires systematic thought, strong listening skills and comprehensive synthesis. Wordy and detailed notes can often becoming disorganized without headers or keywords and phrases. Lacking a system of abbreviations, symbols and indexing will compound this problem.

## 5 Common Mistakes Of Note-taking

The top five mistakes in note-taking are:

1. Attempting to transcribe word for word and failure to summarize
2. Keeping notes in different places (disorganization)
3. Not asking for clarification, repetition or to slow down
4. Losing the general theme or topic due to inappropriate or missing headings, sub-headings, and keywords
5. Writing so quickly that the notes are illegible

Before you learn to take notes, you must learn to listen. How to listen effectively? This is covered in Chapter 3.

When you are taking notes, you want to listen for the most important information, for cause and effect, and main, sub and supporting details. This requires that you listen for information, with an understanding of how information and knowledge is classified and presented. Highlighting and underlining, much like headings and sub-headings can help you keep track of general themes and ideas.  However, over highlighting can detract you from the validity and usability of your notes. Furthermore, the Association for Psychological Sciences ranked highlighting and underlining low as a learning strategy.  However, it may be useful in the organization and therefore the future access of your notes.

Highlighting may draw attention to individual facts and away from making connections and inferences, however it is useful in project management or other information gathering contexts.  What can you do besides highlighting?  Make your notes visual. Add symbols as visual cues and this is covered in Chapter 4 in more detail.

# CHAPTER 3

# BETTER LISTENING EQUALS BETTER NOTE-TAKING

Listening is an essential skill in note-taking and not just when learning.

There are three modes of acquiring knowledge -- listening, seeing and doing. As children, we learn to speak, walk, and gain independence by observation alone. If eighty percent of what you know is learned by listening, then you must learn to listen effectively. You can develop and strengthen your listening skills through the constant application of thoughtful preparation and engagement.

**Preparation**

The first part of listening is preparation: familiarize yourself with the material of discussion and determine the main ideas and important details.

During any lecture or presentation, the first slide is usually a brief introduction of what will be covered during the presentation. So, take note as this will prepare you for what to come in the lecture. Or the lecturer may say things like:

*"Today, we will learn about xxxxxxx"* or

*"In this lecture, I will cover....."*

These are verbal clues that you must take note of to prepare yourself for the information to be delivered.

If you know what is to be covered before a lecture or presentation, then you may come prepared with questions as this will facilitate more active-listening and gather more attention.

It's very easy not to listen well. The topic is boring. You don't like the subject. Or, the speaker is taking a position which you don't agree. There may be distractions during the lecture like someone talking while the lecture is in progress or noises from outside the classroom.

Maybe you are listening, but you are only listening for details and not central ideas so your understanding is limited. If you are excessively emotional or resistant to new ideas, even if you are listening, you are less likely to receive the entire message. Withhold any bias or judgment you have until the entire message has been communicated. If you have a pre-set idea of what you'll hear, then you will only hear the parts that confirm what you already believe. Keep an open mind, being thoughtful instead of overly critical judging the content and not the delivery.

## How Information Is Presented

Most information is presented in the 5Ws structure. When you read a newspaper report, you will find this familiar. The 5Ws+H are popular in journalism, research and report writing.

The 5Ws are:

1. **Who** was involved?
2. **What** happened?
3. **Why** did that happen?
4. **Where** did it take place?
5. **When** did it take place?
6. **How** did it happen?

In most cases, your notes should cover these six basic questions necessary for information gathering.

With this in mind, you should always ask:

**What is the information?**

**Who? Where? When? How?**

**And, don't forget to include why it is important?**

This is where you can add in new connections and synthesis of information. Each question covers facts necessary to include for your notes to be complete. Above all, the answer to these questions is never just yes or no. If your notes answer these six questions, you will have all the information needed to write an accurate report, summary, outline or follow-up questions.

Another way that most information is presented is as follows:

## What – Why – How – Examples

So, if you are teaching about electric motors, it will be:

- **What** is an electric motor?
- **Why** electric motors are important?
- **How** does an electric motor work? Examples and illustrations of applications and use of electric motors or types of electric motors

## Listen Out For Cues From The Lecturer

Your lecturer is not going directly say "you should write this down" or "this is the main idea and the supporting details."

However, you can learn to recognize when a speaker is making an important point. They will often pause, change their volume or pitch, repeat the main idea, and give visual cues with body language, sharing graphics or writing key words or phrases.

They will also spend more time talking about their most important points or actively engage the listeners by asking questions, inviting participation in an activity, demonstration or writing exercise. They will also give examples, repeat the main idea, and cite other sources to justify their claims. And, they may use direct statements and signal words. A good speaker will introduce their main ideas and then follow with supporting material.

Listen for these kinds of phrases that signal a preface or introduction:

*"There are three reasons why...." (HERE THEY COME!)*

*"First...Second... Third...." (THERE THEY ARE!)*

*"And most important,...." (A MAIN IDEA!)*

*"A major development...." (A MAIN IDEA AGAIN!)*

*"Let me give you an example...."(illustration to a main idea)*

This will give you an idea of where the speaker is headed and thus a general structure for your notes. The speaker will then share their supporting material and signal with phrases like:

*"For example...." and "As an example..."*

*"For instance...."*

*"Similarly...." or "In contrast..."*

*"Also...." and "Next..."*

*"Further...." and "Futhermore..."*

*"On the other hand...."*

*"On the contrary...."*

She may signal directly with:

*"Now this is important…."*

*"Remember that…."*

*"The important idea is that…."*

*"The basic concept here is…."*

And, finally, he may signal conclusion or summary with transition words like:

*"Therefore…."*

*"In conclusion…."*

*"As a result…."*

*"Finally…."*

*"In summary…."*

*"From this we see…."*

Understanding how information is presented will improve the value of your notes. When you are listening and taking notes, it is helpful to ask yourself:

*What is the main idea?*

*What are the supporting details?*

The outline method can help you keep track of key concepts and focus your notes on relevant information. While other methods like the Cornell method will engage you by helping you ask questions so you will be listening for the answer. Who? What? Where? When?

How? Concept maps will also help you make connections: Are there any connections between this information and what I already know? How does this information connects with the previous? And, listen for signal words that speakers use to frame their message and keep in touch with their listeners. You can use the same signal words the speaker uses to structure their thoughts as you write your notes.

# CHAPTER 4

# EFFECTIVE NOTE-TAKING TECHNIQUES

The worst method for taking notes is to have a piece of blank paper with texts all over the place with no columns, no lines and no visual cues.

Don't make this mistake. This chapter will teach you the right note-taking skills that will help you to better organize information to revise and recall.

There are several different note-taking strategies covered in this book. In the first part of this section, we will focus on what the strategy is and how and when to use it as well as the pros and cons. The latter part of this chapter will provide an overview of symbols, visual cues and abbreviations. The ability to fluently use shorthand will help you to successfully take a large quantity notes that are readable for future use.

# Part 1: Different note-taking strategies

## Cornell Note-taking System

This method systematically condenses and organizes your notes prior to any revision or recopying. Walter Pauk, reading and study center director of Cornell University, developed this style of note-taking in his work in developmental education and study skills. Cornell technique allows you to organize and make connections during the note-taking process. You partition your notes prior to writing anything down so that there is a 2-3 inch margin on the left and a large writing space for information on the right.

As you move forward, skip a few lines between main points so as to complete phrases and sentences later. In the margin on the left, label each idea and detail with a keyword. This will allow you later to review at a glance, reference or test yourself, depending on the purpose of your notes whether from a meeting or for an online course. You can also record the date, names of key people in the topic, or events. After synthesizing the information as a whole, you can put the essential question into words and summarize, make connections or add any other comments into your notes.

This format is great for drawing out important concepts and ideas. It is simple and efficient, reducing the need for revision and thus saving time and effort. This can be used in any lecture situation and applied to most professional purposes.

See sample below:

| Subject: | | Date: |
|---|---|---|
| **Topic / Title :** | | |
| Questions | Your Notes Here: | |
| **Summary:** | | |

Cornell

Write:
- questions
- Keyword
- Event
- People
- bright idea you have

Write your notes here on this space.

SUMMARY: Summarize your topic here.

## The Outlining Method

*[Hand-drawn outline template showing:]*

*Outline*

Date: [____] Topic: [____]

Main Point: _____

Sub Point:
 o _____
 o _____
 o _____
 o _____

Main Idea: _____
Supporting Idea: _____
 • _____
 • _____
 o _____
 o _____

*Summary*

You can outline your notes organizing main points and supporting details by spacing and indenting each specific point. The distance from the main point indicates how important each specific point is. You can label each point with Roman numerals, letters or decimals. However, labeling each point is insignificant as the spacing indicates the major and minor points.

If you pick an outline style and stick to it, as long as your outline is well categorized and organized, you can use whichever lettering or number system you like. The most general information begins at the left and each fact or detail is indented as it because more specific. Like with the Cornell Note-taking System, you can also record objectives at the beginning and summary or additional comments or questions at the end.

When done right, this system is highly organized recording content as well as relationships. This system is ideal for high content and information presentations that already have an outline organization whether supporting major points with details or building up to major points with details. However, if the meeting or presentation is non-linear or otherwise organized, this format may not be suitable for your needs or note-taking ability. You need enough time to think through and make decisions about the organization of your notes when outlining.

## T-Charts and 3-Column Charts

If the information can be previously organized into distinct categories, taking notes in a chart or graphic organizer can help you track ideas, reduce writing, and see comparisons and relationships. You can set up your paper by drawing columns and labeling each with an appropriate heading. You then record words, phrases and main ideas under the appropriate category, thus sorting information as you take notes.

## When Do You Use T-Charts?

T-charts are ideal for examining two sides of a topic. For example, the topic may be the advantages and disadvantages of using iPads for young kids.

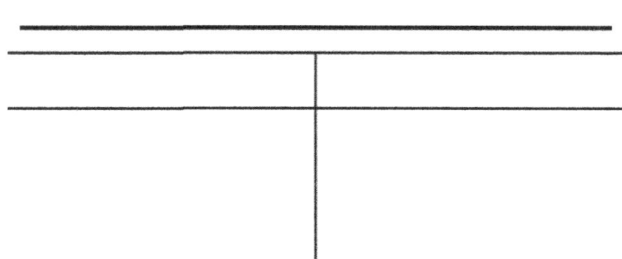

It can also be used for comparing two subjects of study. For example the difference between Theory X and Theory Y or the difference between Model A and Model B.

So, listen to the lecture carefully, if you hear the teacher starts to make comparison, get your pen ready to draw a T-chart.

- Fact and Opinion
- Myths and Facts
- Advantages and Disadvantages
- Strengths and Weaknesses
- Pros and Cons
- Past and Present
- Cause and Effect
- Problem and Solution
- Examples and Non-Examples

It highlights the comparison of problems and solutions, examples and non-examples, and before-and-after. If you are evaluating the performance of the presentation you can chart areas of strengths and areas of improvement, but if you are focused on the content you can pair one salient detail on the right with a main idea on the left. T-charts are also good for question and answer or word and definition/visual representations.

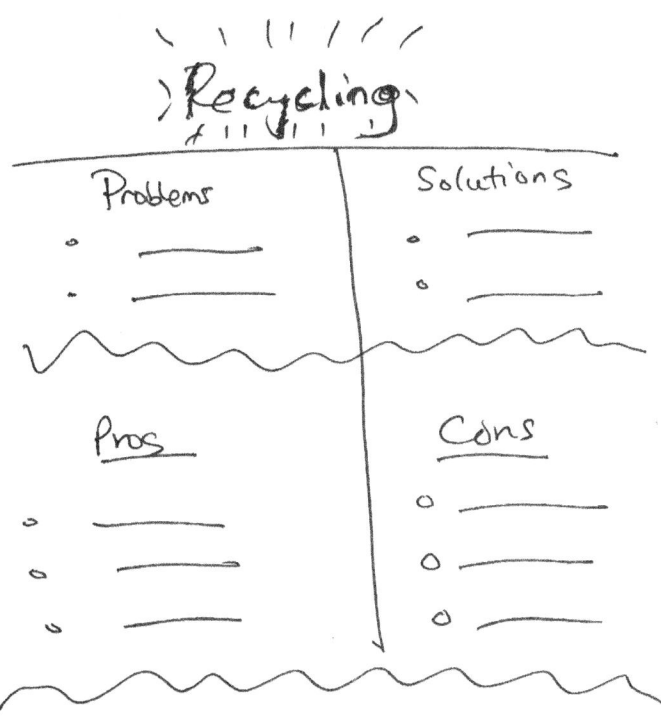

If you are exploring multiple topics, 3-column notes might be more appropriate. Like the T-chart, 3-column chart adapts the Cornell Note-taking System by organizing content by information type. As in the Cornell method, the first column contains the main topic or keyword and in the second column supporting details. However, in the third column, you note your own connections, observations thoughts and opinions or even questions you have.

You may also adapt the columns for other purposes, but do not neglect the third column as it reveals how actively you were engaged and listening. You can also use charts to organize your thinking as you record information or track conversation and dialogue. It is essential to appropriately categorize the information and use the system to your advantage without losing the overview of the entire sequence of discussion.

For example, the teacher may say, there are three components of good note-taking. So, you can draw 3 columns and capture the points said for each component in each column.

|  |  |  |
|--|--|--|
|  |  |  |

## The Concept Mapping Method

Concept Maps are diagrams of major points and significant sub-points reflecting relationships, like sequence and cause-and-effect. These kinds of visual graphic organizers show how each fact or idea relates to another fact or idea. It is a graphic representation of the content of a lecture or presentation, drawing an overall picture. It requires active engagement with the content and critical thinking, but it reflects immediate knowledge and understanding. It can also be a strong reinforcement for visual thinkers by grouping or organizing material in a highly visual representation. Organizing material by relationships and importance, concept maps can be used as a quick reference as an overview or guide in recalling the discussion.

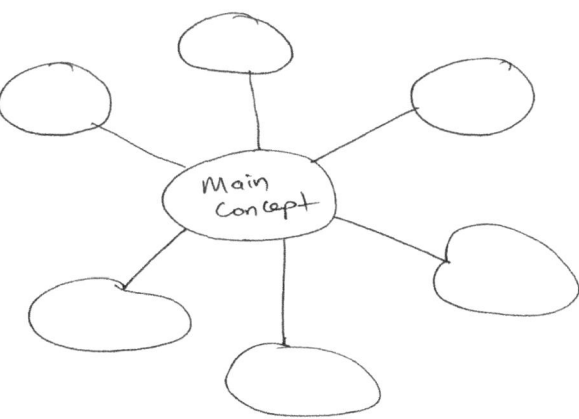

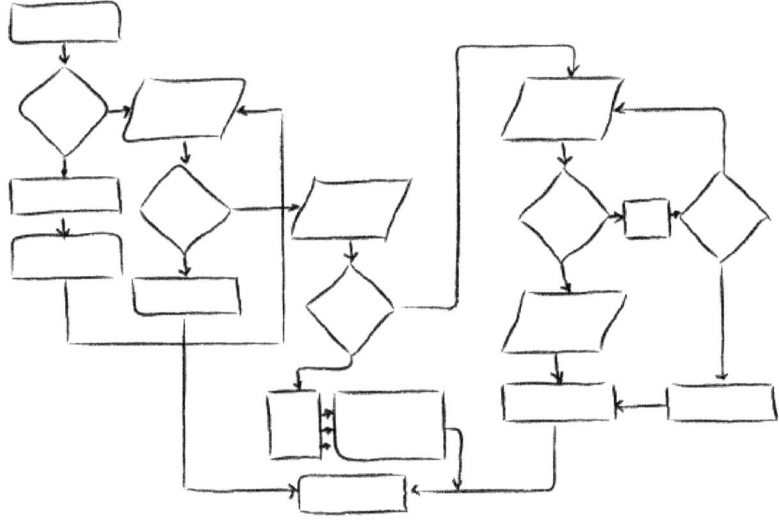

Concept maps are not restricted to one pattern. While circles or boxes are often used, you may use a variety of creative shapes and arrows or lines as long as they are useful and significant for you and others who might use your notes. You will most likely be successful using concept maps when the content is heavy and well-organized. They can be easily annotated or edited by adding numbers, marks and color coding. Most importantly, this format allows you to visually track the presentation or lecture. However, you may miss shifts in content from major points to facts and supporting details. Concept maps may also require more organization in meetings or consultations with no pre-set agenda or multiple speakers contribute to the discussion.

A concept map is a two-dimensional diagram that contains concepts that are often circle and directional named links that are usually arrows. It reveals the understanding and knowledge speaker of the listener. It also facilitates the mental structure of long term memory which is structured through hierarchical clusters. The most general concepts are usually at the top of the hierarchy and the general concepts are arranged by significance below. However, the clusters may interconnect as in a flow chart. In general, it visually outlines the content.

However, a concept map can be as simple as a spider map. You circle the subject or topic in the middle of the page, writing the main ideas that the support the topic on lines radiating from the central idea. And, then you include significant details on the lines attached to the main idea. Concept maps can also be inserted into outlines or Cornell Style notes as well.

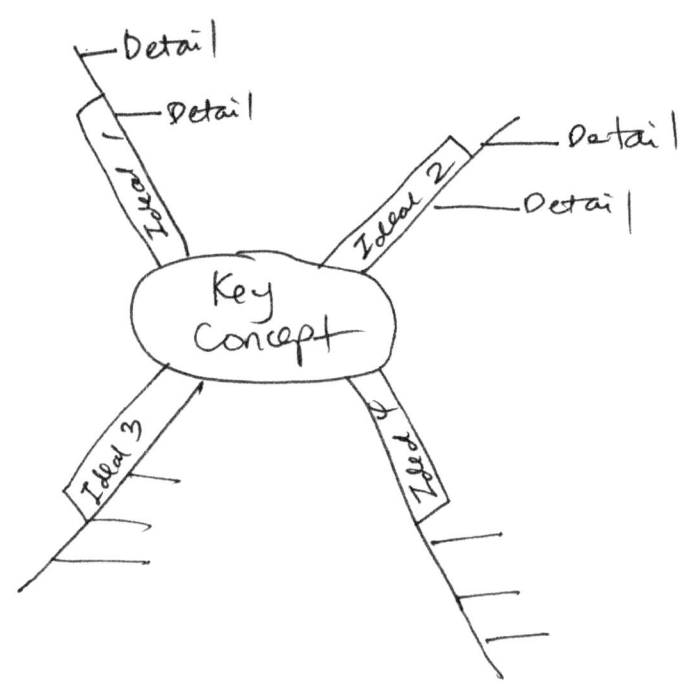

## Fishbone Map

The last concept map we will discuss is the fishbone concept map that Kaurou Ishikawa began using in Japan in the 1950s to visually work out the possible causes of a problem. It identifies possible causes by category branching off like the bones of a fish. The head should identify the problem or issue further explained in the backbone of the fish. The first four bones of the fish are the four main causes that contribute to the problem. As you brainstorm around each cause, you can document contributing factors or details, breaking down each cause until you have identified the root causes.

Cause mapping is similar in that it focuses more specifically on cause-and-effect analysis looking at root causes instead of specific causes. It can also focus the conversation in brainstorming sessions because it allows you to rate potential causes by importance and diagram this hierarchically. It, however, can be modified for main points and supporting details.

Regardless of your preferred note-taking style, it is important to be well-versed in all of your note-taking options. You may choose to insert a concept map into your Cornell style notes or break up your outline with a 3-column chart. A fishbone diagram may be very beneficial in a small meeting but a T-chart might be more appropriate for evaluating the strength and weakness of a particular program or policy. Having a variety of strategies in your note-taking repertoire will allow you to make more efficient choices in your notes and reduce wasted productivity.

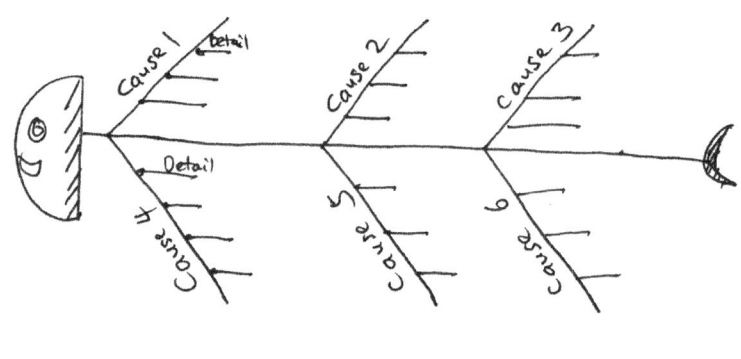

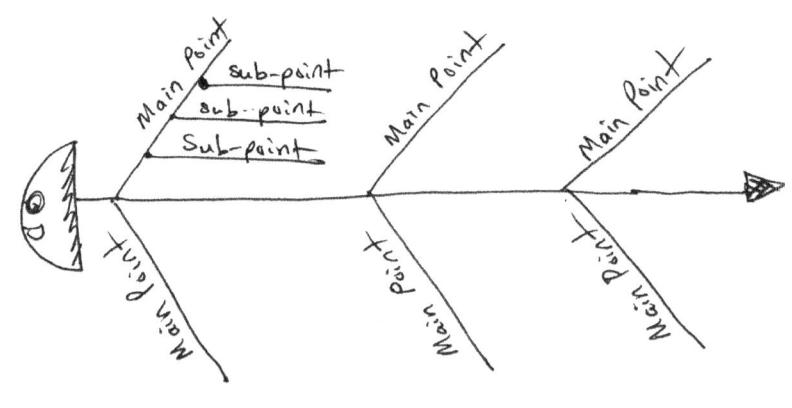

## Part 2: Use symbols and abbreviations in your notes

The use of symbols and abbreviations is useful when speed is essential. However, for your shorthand to be practical, you need to consistently use the same symbols and abbreviations so that you are familiar with symbols frequently used in your courses. You should develop a system of symbols and abbreviations; some personal, and some specific to the context. But, be consistent when using symbols and abbreviations. This will increase the usability and thus value of your notes.

Some common symbols include the equal sign, dots and areas. Various symbols come from mathematics like equal and less than or greater than. The symbol for therefore was first used in mathematical proofs in the 1600s.

Abbreviations, on the other hand, may be common, personal or discipline-specific. For example, three notes in a downward triangle is the mathematical symbol for because, but b/c is also a common abbreviation. Just as many shorthand symbols are commonly used in mathematics, most common abbreviations have roots in Latin. But, you may wish to shorten any word that is commonly used in your lectures and meetings. And, of course, you should use any discipline-specific abbreviation that you and others perusing your notes will understand. Some abbreviations are so well known and widely used that they have become an Acronym - an abbreviation pronounced as a word. For example, the word 'laser' was originally an abbreviation for 'Light Amplification by Stimulation Emission of Radiation'. It now is a noun in its own right. The following provide symbols and abbreviations for your use.

## Symbols for Note-Taking

=     equals/is equal to/is the same as

≠     is not equal to/is not the same as

≡     is equivalent to

∴     therefore, thus, so

∵     Because

+     and, more, plus

>     more than, greater than

<     less than

−     less, minus

→     gives, causes, produces, leads to, results in, is given by, is produced by, results from, comes from

↗     rises, increases by

↘ falls, decreases by

α proportional to

α̸ not proportional to

## Abbreviations for Note-Taking

| Common Abbreviations | Personal Abbreviations |
|---|---|
| i.e. (id est) = that is<br><br>e.g (exempla grate) = for example<br><br>NB (nota benne) =note well<br><br>no. (numero) = number<br><br>c.f. (confer) = compare<br><br>etc. (et cetera)= and so on | In the case of quantities and concepts, these are represented by Greek letters in many fields - A or a (alpha) B or b (beta)<br><br>You can use the scientific abbreviations for elements, such as Au for gold, Mg for magnesium, H2O for water and NaCl for salt. |

## More Short Forms

**@ - at**

**0 - degree**

**# - number**

**% - percent**

**$ - dollar**

**yr - year**

**lb - pound**

**w/ - with**

**w/o - without**

**w/i - within**

**ch - chapter**

**& - and**

**dept - department**

**max - maximum**

**min - minimum**

**gov - government**

**diff - different**

**qn - question**

**wrt - write**

**b/4 - before**

**b/c - because**

**pg - page**

# Part 3: Visual Notes Quick Guide

Why add visual to your notes?

It makes note-taking fun and enables key ideas to stand out from the pages. Visual notes help you to capture, retain and revise more efficiently for your examination. What kind of visuals can you create in your notes? Here are some basic components.

## Fonts And Styles

You don't really need many font types. At least 2 types of fonts to differentiate between main ideas and sub ideas or header texts and normal texts will be fine.

You don't need to be an artist to be making visual notes. You can also use Capital letters and lower case letters to differentiate texts. For big ideas or key topics, make the letters bold and bigger than the normal texts so, it stands out. If you want to shade the letters, you can always come back and do it later rather than to do it when the teacher is speaking. Just write it bigger first and then come back to touch up. You don't want to waste time adding shading and then missed out important points of the lesson. Once you decided on your font type, stick to it and be consistent.

Another way to emphasize is to use a bigger point size pen or a different color

For main idea or key idea, you want to emphasize it. You can emphasize it by using a different font style from your usual writing style. You can write bigger by increasing the font size and make it bold. For example:

# ABCDEFGHIJK

You can also make an outline of the text like this:

Or add a shadow or shade the letters, like this:

abcdefghijklmnopqrstuvwxyz

Once you decided on the font style, stick to it and use it consistently in your notes. Remember that you can come back to the notes and add shadow or shade it later if you need to move on to take down other points during the lecture.

## Bullets

There are different ways to take down points as bulleted texts. You can have a variety like this:

## Frames, Shapes And Bubbles

Shapes like circle, oval, square and rectangle or cloud bubbles are called frames or containers.

You place texts in a frame or a bubble to highlight a central idea or concept. It is also used to separate a concept or key idea so that it stands out from other texts. It is also another way to emphasize something when used with a certain font type.

If you hear a good quote, draw a cloud bubble around it. If someone said something really important, put it inside a speech bubble.

Here are some examples of clouds and bubbles:

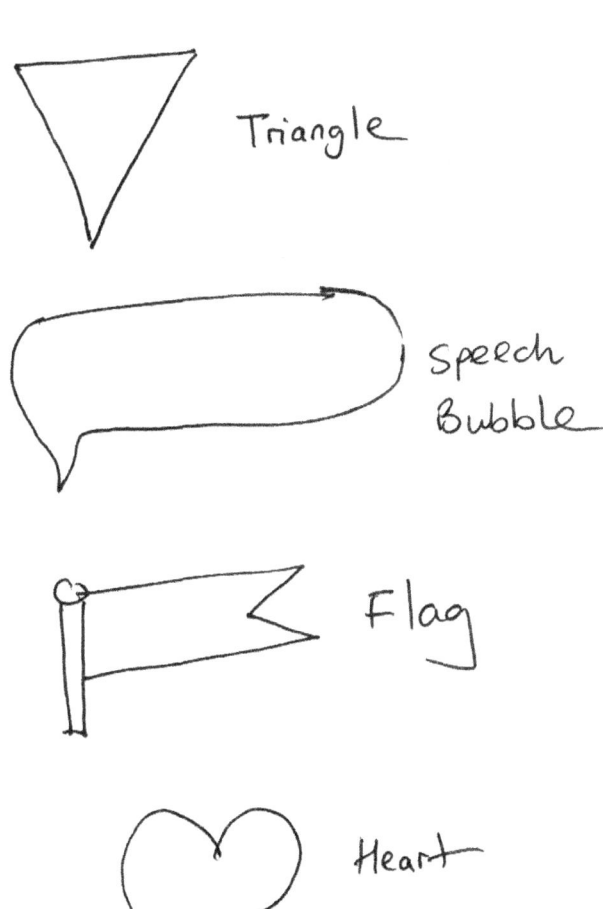

Triangle

Speech Bubble

Flag

Heart

## Arrows For Flow and Steps and Connectors and Links

Arrows and lines or connectors are to show how one idea leads to another or to show a sequence of events or steps.

See examples below.

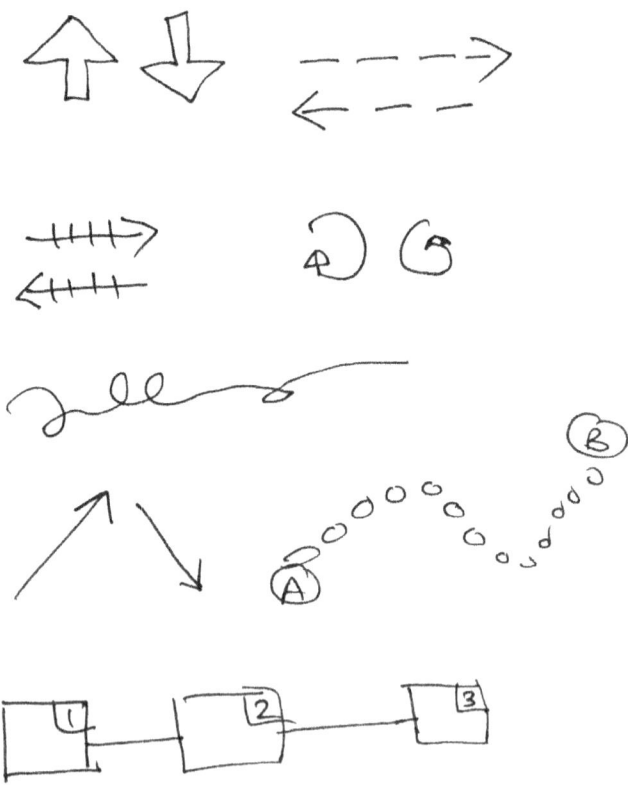

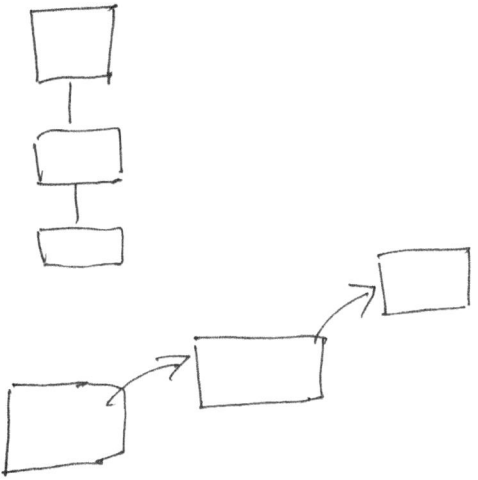

## Symbols

The next component is to use symbols or icons as sign-posting. It helps you to spot key information at a glance for example the date of a major event, books to read and references for further studying. Create your own set of icon library and draw these icons or symbols at the end of your note book. Once you created them, use it consistently.

What are some icons or symbols and their meanings that you can use?

Here are some icons and meanings for your reference. You are free to create your own icons for your own purposes.

 - book to read
  read up

 - search
- look up

 - place
- location

 - web
- internet

 - questions asked by teachers
-questions you have

 - sudden inspiration
-sudden great idea

 - good idea
-good point

 - challenge / conflict
- negative event / crisis

 - problem solved
- positive event or outcome

 - deadline
- time or period

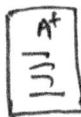 - exam topic

 - costing or information related to monetary value

 - danger

 - very important
- very hot

   - important people or name

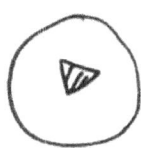   - video to watch

Develop your own key icons that make sense to you. When you have done that, use the last few pages of your note book and draw each icon and their meanings at the back as a legend or call it an Icon Library.

## Apply Shading & Color

If you want to add more color to your notes, then you can use a different color pen for header texts or for emphasis and a black or blue pen for normal text. The other way is to use a highlighter to add shadows to give depth to the black and white sketches. Use the highlighter and go over the base or the side of an object. Pick one color for your shadows. But do not over use too many colors if not, you may make your notes too messy. See example below.

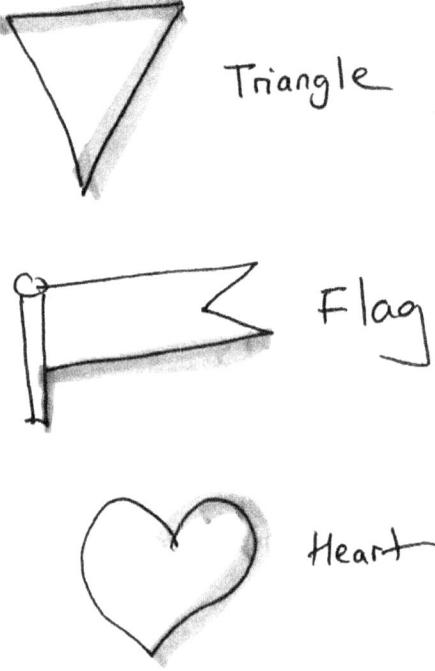

## Practice Makes Perfect

Don't expect to be perfect when you first try out these new note-taking strategies. Through practice, you will make excellent notes.

# CHAPTER 5

# WHAT TO DO WITH THE FIRST AND LAST FEW PAGES OF YOUR NOTEBOOK?

This chapter teaches you how to create a reference for the notes you have taken. The first type of reference is the contents page. The content page tells you what topic appears on which page inside your note book.

The second type of reference is the Icon Library page. Draw your icons and write down the meaning of each icon on the page.

You have learnt about writing down keywords when using Cornell note-taking technique. Now, you can consolidate all the important keywords and write them down at the back of the note book together with the page number that it appears like an index. This will help you to find the information you need quickly. The keyword tags are optional but at least you should have a content page and an icon listing page.

## Contents Page And Page Numbering

When you buy a new note book, leave the first 6 pages blank. Do not start writing on the first page. The first 6 pages are reserved to be used as content page after you have used up the pages of your note book.

You must also leave at least 10 pages or more at the back of your new note book for your image icon legend or keyword tags. Write down all the important keywords and the page number that the word appears inside the note book pages for easy reference. You can arrange the keywords in alphabetical order if you like. Remember to number your notebook after you have completed using the note book.

# CONTENTS

Cycles in plants and animals
 (Life cycles)     10
Magnets     20
Human system (Digestive system)     25

# My Icons

 Books to refer

 Look up

 Important location

 Internet website

 Questions for teachers

Keyword Tags

A:
atom - 13, atmoshpere - 23, atomic energy 35,

B:
biosphere -44, boiling point - 65

# RESOURCES

## Types Of Pens:

You will need a bigger point size pen of at least 0.7mm to 1.0 mm to make nicer notes. The bigger tip also makes shading easier and frames more prominent.

**Pilot G2 Retractable Premium Gel Ink Roller Ball Pens (0.7mm)**

http://amzn.to/22JAqNg

# Pilot G2 Retractable Premium Gel Ink Roller Ball Pens, Bold Point, Assorted Colors (1.0mm)

http://amzn.to/1qVa537

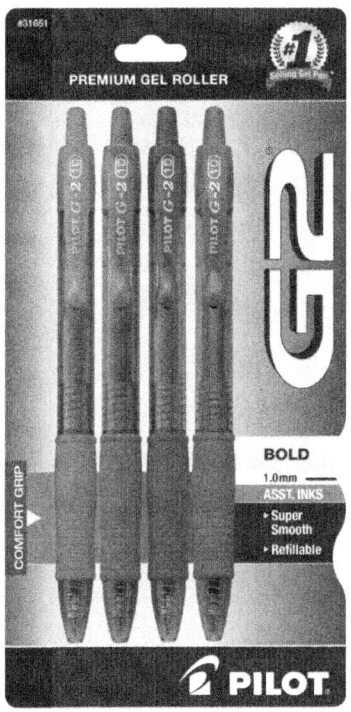

## Retractable Highlighters

It is hard to find retractable highlighter and I find this really cool. This saves you time trying to cap and uncap when you are rushing to take down the notes.

http://amzn.to/1qVbw1j

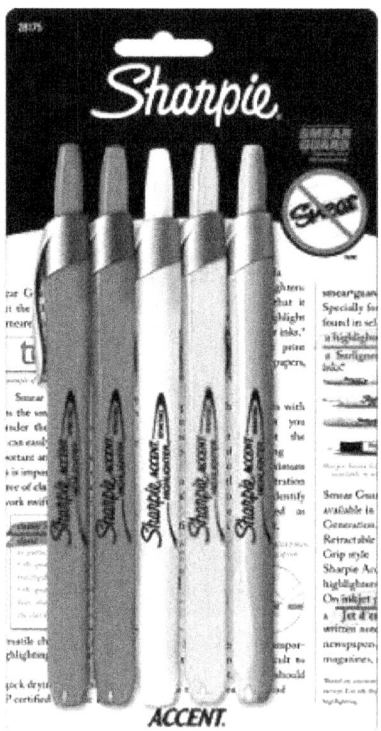

## FREE Advance Visual Notes Online Video Lessons

Go to:

http://braindoodles.net/

Here you can find free doodle lessons for those who want to do some serious and advance techniques in drawing visual notes.

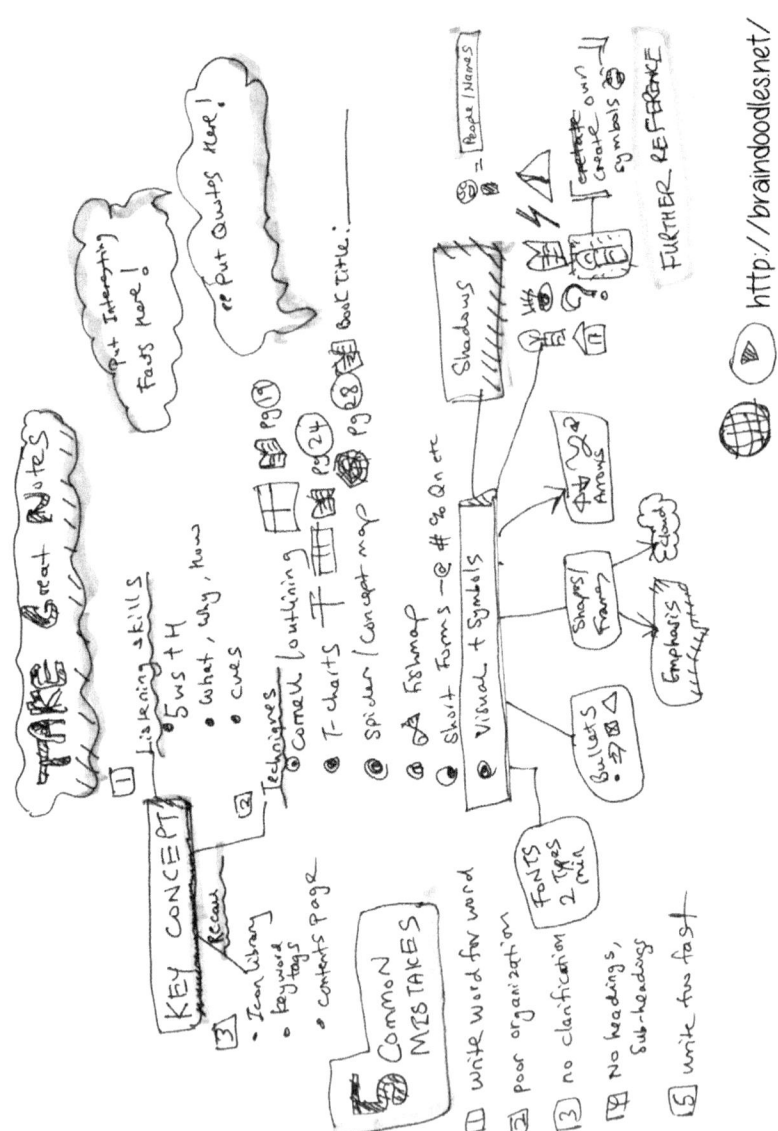

Printed in Great Britain
by Amazon